Stages
Poems of a Life Cycle

by
Rita Ben-Or

LAURIAT PRESS
PITTSBURGH, PENNSYLVANIA 15222

ISBN # 0-8059-9055-0
ISBN-13 # 978-0-8059-9055-3
Library of Congress Control Number: 2005931653
Printed in the United States of America

First Printing

For information or to order additional books, please write:
Lauriat Press
701 Smithfield St.
Pittsburgh, PA 15222
U.S.A.
1-800-834-1803
Or visit our web site and
on-line bookstore at www.lauriatpublishing.com

Table of Contents

Foreword

A Parable For Our Times
By Rita Ben-Or

Ant: (To Grasshopper)
"All summer long you sang while I worked - and now that winter approaches you want to borrow grain? I worked for my grain while you sang - now, come winter, I'll reap the rewards of my work - while you - why this time you can dance!"*

So the grasshopper starved until she was at Death's door, whereupon she summoned all the other grasshoppers in the land and said:

"Singing is a futile pursuit. While it indeed brings you pleasure it brings you no food - and the ants of this world are not willing to depart with their hard-earned grain to listen to your voices. So forget about singing, and instead gather grain." and thus saying, she died.

The other grasshoppers gathered round her body and vowed to the last one to heed their late compatriots advice. They all began to gather grain, though they were ill suited to it by nature, and much of the grain spilled and rotted. They managed to become barely competent grain gatherers - enough so that they didn't starve.

In the meantime there was less grain for the ants to gather efficiently - and all the singing of the land stopped. The only sound that could be heard was the scuttling of workers' feet. Life for all was the gathering of grain so one could eat and thereby live and therefore gather more grain. The very **raison d'etre** of life was simply perpetuation - an endless, meaningless cycle; for the voices of the land, the song of the spirit, was dead.

*(From **Les Fables de La Fontaine**,*
freely translated from the French by Rita Ben-Or)

I. Childhood

Rhyme Discovery

Give me some pie
So I won't cry!

And It Fits Into Verse!

The Grandpa Clock

The Grandpa Clock that's on the wall
Never walks or talks at all,
But stands there ticking all the day
Watching little children play.

He lets the people know the hour
When to bathe and when to shower,
When to water their best flower,
When to wake and when to rest.
When to dress their very best.

Pretty, big, old Grandpa Clock
Knows just when to tick-tick-tock!

Winter Wedding

The snow is falling, gently, gently,
Soft and silent to the ground.
The earth, her bridal dress is donning,
White and glistening all around.

Mother elm her bark is primping
And the lake, a mirror serves.
Sister Christmas tree is making
Vanilla flavored snow preserves.

All is calm and still and quiet
And the blessings have been said.
Father North Wind plays the music;
Winter and the World are wed!

II. Adolescence

And Yet a Universe Became!

There was nothing, nothing -
And yet a universe became.
There was no space.
There was no earth to fill the space.
There was no sun to warm the earth
And spit out planets as it spun
To keep their course in endless time
And follow constant in a path
Set down for them by their creator.
There were no worlds to sit in air -
There was no air;
No massive forms of density,
No gray lumps of oozing dampness
Nor veils of ghostly moving spray
That formed in misty vagueness
Without dimension or solid shape.

There was nothing, nothing -
And yet a universe became.
There was no rain.
No water streamed from soft, drenched skies
Or dribbled slowly down
From slight discolorations in the heavens.
Nor did it freeze to icy pellets
That slowly grew and crashed
Destroying what they mashed below.
No snow was there to fall fainting from the sky
Transforming all on which it fell to only whiteness.
There was no whiteness.

There was nothing, nothing -
And yet a universe became.
There was no startling daylight;
No flashing light that showed the way,
That showed the world.
There was no world.

There was no deep pitched darkness
That seeped in slowly until it formed
One wholeness of blackness and pure quiet.
There was no quiet.
No softness and no stillness
To lie like a deep cushion and cover up all sound;
No crashing loudness, splintering, cracking;
No steady dull booming thunder tramping,
No shrill ripping screaming,
No soft cooing caresses,
No rustling sweet tones.

There was nothing, nothing -
And yet a universe became.
There was no ugliness, twisted and disfigured,
No horror no revulsion;
No beauty, gentle, rhythmic and pulsating,
No beauty by which to temper ugliness.
And even terror there was not
To gouge with ripping claws,
To make the blood of life turn black.
And even peace there was not
To settle the terror like a soothing mother
To make the blood run red again
And knotted fear be happiness.

There was nothing, nothing -
And yet a universe became.
And yet space formed out of nothing -
Space enough to hold skies,
To hold the air to blue the skies.
Space enough for light
For a molten mass of hugeness
Of burning, boiling gas to give off light;
To hurl planets into space and warm them
And still to not come close enough and chill them.
Space enough to hold a million whirling balls
Small in their comparison
But overwhelming hugeness when measured by themselves.
Space enough to keep these massive bodies spinning
And yet never come quite near enough
To fear collision.

Space enough to hold a massive
Atmosphere of spreading emptiness.
And even space was there to hold
A sea of water that fell and formed a sea on earth.
And still more space to sprinkle droplets
That made no difference to the moving waters
But gently washed the boiling bodies
Until they formed to solid matter.
And still was water left
To freeze into huge stones
And pock mark the masses below.
And snow fell to cover those marks
And cool them with a sweet moist touch -
And there became whiteness.

There was nothing, nothing -
And yet a universe became.
And yet light streaked the new made sky
And shone in brilliance on the worlds.
And some of those worlds in answer
Twinkled back - And there were stars.
And to one side where the light
Could not reach the worlds would turn
When they tired of this brightness -
And there was dark.
This dark it filled up slowly
Till the rolling worlds turned softly
And quiet seeped in everywhere.
And then as quiet came too much
There was defiance and the heavens boomed
And noise became - crackling lightning
And dull thudding thunder;
Shrieking winds and chortling breezes;
Sweet sounds, soft gurgling splashes.

There was nothing, nothing -
And yet a universe became.
And yet as the worlds formed
And the light pointed out the worlds
And stars twinkled in the darkness,
Sweet sounds sang to the stars
And lo, there was beauty - the first beauty,
Tender and painfully wonderful,
Showing itself suddenly, completely.

And where the worlds turned away
There was ugliness, huge and overpowering,
Steady with horror and bleakness.
And this caused terror to emanate fearfully,
Strongly out into space.
But horror must not be.
And so the light shone through
Painting a path for beauty.
And beauty stepped in and kissed away
The most of horror, and smoothed
Some wrinkled brows of fear -
And there was peace.

There was nothing, nothing -
And yet a universe became.
And yet the sun and world and space and air,
Cold and heat and water and ice,
Snow and light and day and dark,
Quiet and noise, and beauty and ugliness,
Terror and peace, fear and hope,
All combined to form a life -
Throbbing, vibrating, pulsating life.
Life and power, life and people.
People and power, power and strength.
And the people themselves became creators.
And the people themselves became destroyers.
There was nothing, nothing -
And yet a universe became!

Opportunities Not Taken

(or Fifteen Years Old - And What Have I Accomplished?)

The sun has set
The day is done
And one must sleep.
A seed lies rotting in the deep
Not even having sent a green shoot
Groping out into the sun -
And life is done.

New York

(First prize contest winner, "Portrait of New York")

This is New York,
These are the people of New York,
These are the dreams of the people;
Concrete bodies with bones of steel,
Monuments to the sweating man, the creating man -
Sweating over steel, creating a dream.

Burning eyes like plates of gold,
Burning with the fever of man's ambition.
High heads wearing the clouds, wearing the sky;
Breathing thick black breath into the sky,
Blowing slim fine smoke out at the sky.

We have made you, New York
We have made you from scraps of molten iron.
We have made you from sand and mud and water,
We have made you from melted ore and pewter.
We have made you with body oil, body grime, body power.

We have built you with human passion, city.
We have built you with human soul, city.
We have loved you and built you with human laughter.

And now you can stand, New York,
Work of a hundred years,
Evolution of a thousand peoples,
Offspring of the wedded dreams of millions.
You are a child from the womb of creation
Fathered by the yearnings of seven continents.
You are the heartbeat of a nation, New York.
You are the pulse of America.

A Melody

A silver stream, a blade of grass,
Somewhere beyond a dream, a whippoorwill;
A hollow reed, a rushing breeze,
One note tumbling from the trees
And bouncing down, and soon is lost.
Dancing lights in darker glens
Fragments of a poet's thoughts.
Upon the rushes a bit of human soul
A bit of elfin joy
A creature sits and plays upon a reed
And laughs.

First Love

Why do I say it now?
Why do I say I love you?
Before your ears were near my lips,
Your skin was at my finger tips,
And as I breathed I drank your breath
Yet not a word I told you.

Why am I wishing now?
Why did I not wish with you?
Your mouth had shaped a million dreams,
My mouth was sealed by fear it seams,
And yet my hands could hold you.

Why am I crying now?
My voice was silent near you.
And though I had the fullest breast
My aching throat could find no rest
And only arms enfold you.

Why do I whisper now?
My breath was deep within me.
The words that came past not my teeth.
They fell and rested way beneath
And let my fingers mold you.

But how I say it now!
Please listen! Yes, I love you!
My words fall free, yet now I stand
With empty arms and open hand.
My God! I could have told you!

Eulogy - A Mother's Death

Between two worlds there spans one thought
Between two lives the cord is taut
Two minds may dwell
Two souls may touch
Forever in reality

No heart should break
No friendship end
When touch no longer satisfies
For the mind has eyes
And memory has longer vision

Because I cannot tell you where
I cannot name the place or plan
I tell you that I know you are
Because you are
Because I am

III. Young Adulthood

And One Must Work

And One Must Work
Or read the daily news and do and do
Stepping round the half-seen shadows, brightly, brightly,
Turning on the silent sound of many things
That suffocate the static throb so lightly.

And sit in hundred-watt-illuminated night
To say in block print thus and so is thus and so
And douse the boiling thought with icy drink
Returning slowly to the root the blood warm flow.

With calisthenic joy our day begins,
The twilight hours' dreams are faintly tasted.
And faintly sticky still upon our tongues
The twilight's untapped nectar's wasted.

And how much time,
And how much time it takes
Deliberating on our well-drawn loops.
Column grows on column day by day,
And oh, the endless circling of our groups!

Impatience

Stone upon stone, and dirt dull glass,
Block after block, stone upon stone.
Cracked cement is a bed for trash
In a little boy's plot in a city back yard.

The gusts of spring carry the dust
Of cracked cement and gravel lots,
Of sifting coal, of lumber yards,
Of trash filled cans and empty streets,
And fling it against the dirt dull glass,
a thin, dry hail on the windowpane;
And skim it over the endless blocks
In whirling cones of stinging gray.

The drizzle of spring that drips down pipes
To rusty puddles on the street,
That seeps in dreary drops through grates
Of subway stations underneath;
That clothes the day in gray and black
And middling shades of black and gray;
And slides and trickles over stone -
Stone upon stone and mud streaked glass.

The hard high sun of a city spring
Shines on everlasting brick,
Glints on broken tinted glass
And greasy rainbows left by trucks.
Beams of dust in an empty store
Make fuzzy spotlights on the shelves
Where the little white specks swarm in the light
and powder the labels on the cans.

Block after block, stone upon stone,
Behind the foggy window panes
People sit and sleep and scratch,
Eat and belch and rub their necks.
Children scream with games of tag
Or boredom or just random rage
And play with the gravel in their yard
Or run some chalk on the cracked cement.

A small boy stares at a window box
Of barren soil as hard as rock
And wonders if a thing will grow
If he sits and waits and dares to hope.
And he sits and waits with a watering can
And squints at the sun and probes the soil
With a tentative touch; soil like rock
In a window box in a city spring.

The sun glares in and the earth is hard
And the watering can grows heavy and cold,
And the little boy leaves to scream with his friends
And scoop up the gravel in the yard.

The spring goes on, the gusts of wind,
The dust, the icy, oozing rain,
And people cross the endless stone
And squint at the blinding sun
Or hide behind the dirty shade
Of a dust filled foggy windowpane.

The little boy's eyes meander past
The barren soil of his window box
When suddenly they come to rest on a yellow bud
With tiny, tender points of green
For leaves, and a little shiny stem.

Amazed, he probes the hard caked earth
and finds his finger sinking in,
For underneath is soft and warm.
The bud is little but it grows.

He fingers first the small, firm stem,
Then pokes the tiny, pale green leaves.
The yellow bud is tightly closed
And will not open to his touch.

He grows impatient and annoyed
And tries to pry the petals down
He wants to see a brilliant bloom
Where nothing ever grew before.

The petals rip beneath his nails.
He grasps the layers underneath
And they too slit and crumple off
Till nothing but the heart remains.
The naked center is exposed
To restless fingers searching still,
And that too soon disintegrates
To yellow dust between his hands.

He wipes his palms on a soiled gray shirt,
Jerks at the stem and throws it out.
He stares once more at the barren soil
And wonders when the dusty wind
Will bring another little seed
To rest in his empty window box;
The dusty wind of a city spring.

Stone upon stone and dirt dull glass,
Block after block, stone upon stone.
Cracked cement is a bed for trash
In a little boy's plot in a city back yard.

IV Adulthood

Concerto For Autumn

Late October licks the mind with burning flames of color;
The blazing bush,
The sudden yellow burst around a corner that tops a tree,
Or blue-red camp light smoldering;
Or the gay belatedness of spring-green young ones
Made greener still behind the gold -
Or pumpkin orange good enough to taste.

The tenderness of new grass, mossy soft
Beneath the brittle leaves before the winter promise -
The one-note "tr-r-ing" of a single cricket
Clear and intimate in the cold bright air.

It is runny-nose cold in the shadows
But the sun warms and softens in the clearings -
A patchy remnant of a summer day.

A baby Tom-cat crashes through the leaves
Because he knows the joy of it;
Black he is - eye-stabbing glossy black
Among the muted mustards.
Flash! Whish! A storm of leaves,
A crunching scurry and he's gone.

A fat-plumed squirrel plays peek-a-boo
And running bases with the branches.
One bird sounds, up somewhere -
It could be anywhere - just up,
A song among the colors.

Where The World Meets

This is where the world meets;
The little town of cobble stones and winding streets,
Of chapel spires and the corner pub,
Of neatly rolling patchwork green.
The scene is pastoral;
Could it be England - or perhaps, the south of France?
The cold wind gales, coarse grasses dance,
The rocky crags, the moss, the gorse,
The yellow and the brown of Scotland -

Or is it Wales;
The coal dust in the air,
The thick pitch smell of burning tar,
Slate roofs, slate streets,
The color, grime, of children's faces -
The giant smoke-filled photographs
In gray and white are places;

Or Newfoundland, or Norway, or any seaport town -
The smell of fish, the foggy reach of sea around,
The clammy bite of nighttime
With it's blurred and welcomed lights?

Or are we now in Switzerland;
Alps, snow, ski-lifts and chalets -
The white world plays, marveling in winter.
And down below the blinding blue of a Geneva lake,
The swan-necked boats, their sails plumed out,
The shout and spray of water sports?

Or sultry beaches, the bikinis,
The glistening bronze of seal-slick bodies,
The lean ease of play-men and their women,
The candy colors of the beach pagodas and the blankets,
And the soothing palms, the balm of lazy air and music,
The cafes - the warm, exciting scent of promise;
Are we strolling the Riviera?
The casinos and the gambling joints;
Is this Monaco?

The writhing nudes,
The milling multitudes, the thickened air
Of incense and of body sweat,
Of sticky sweets and whining wails,
The flies, the fish, the feet,
The prophets in the street:
Is this Morocco?
Or South Africa;
The shanty town, the black and barefoot
And the babes with naked bottoms and ragged gowns;
The dusty streets are made of dirt
And brown folks congregate in tumbled bars
While white folks, gliding through
In cars are only passing by.

Is this the Veldt -
The great and grassy plains
Where wildlife roams in calm seclusion
Permitting the intrusion of the curious or scientific?

Or is this Spain;
The rolling, snapping tongue, the liquid steel,
the converse combination of a silk-sheathed snake,
The sharp report of heal upon a flat wood floor,
The dry, red clay, the baking sun,
And more; the olives and the wine?

Or is it Palestine;
The endless rolling dunes, the plains of death,
The searing breath of desert sands,
The barren lands, the blood-red rocky canyons
Drenched with dying sun, the salt Dead Sea,
Or northward to the Galilee?
Or is this Haifa
Where the winding streets climb to the sky in tiers,
And lights strung as upon a giant, festive tree,
And moonlight peers behind a sky-tipped building;
Or in the Valley of Jesreel,
Is this the rich and fertile land of milk and honey?

Or maybe Hong Kong with its frying smells,
The high pitched yells of merchants in the streets,
The blue jeans and the tiny feet,
The rickshaw and the compact car,
The five tone bells
and folk-rock from a bar that's filled with sailors?

Or have we come to Paris,
With the Avant Garde that flaunt their credo
And defy you with their garb,
Their voices and their speech,
Their pitched emotions that reach for your attention;
Are these the street cafes,
The starving artists come to pitch their tents,
the canvasses lined up along the curb,
The scents and sounds of the creative agony?

Or is this Southern Italy;
The olive faces, the moustaches,
The withered women black-gowned and black-stockinged,
Tongues weaving through the empty spaces,
Toothless, gray haired but undaunted,
The earringed children with their crosses.
Carts of fruits and vegetables pulled by horses,
mutely patient, waiting death?

Or have we a metropolis;
The concrete crags that dwarf us all,
The constant wall,
The artificial air made up of gasoline and smoke,
Or greasy steam from open doors?
We walk the junk-strewn floors,
Electric ceilings are our sky;
Yet here it is, and no one wonders why
The multitudes with hungry souls
Converge to find their reason..

This is where the world meets;
The plains, the mountains, lakes,
The deserts, and the roiling streets;
The compact universe, the sample world -
This is America.

Joy

The sudden spray of children's voices in a silent room.
The sun baking on the damp earth, cooking up the aroma of spring.
Summer bells; tricycle tringle, toy fire engine dong-dong,
The pied-piper ringing of the ice-cream truck.
The snow discovery from a frosted window on an early winter morning.
The smell of any season.

Child's Teacher
"This is not a poem...it doesn't rhyme."

Poetry
Does not have to be
A rhyming bit
of prosery

A poem exalts
It vaults
The common imagery

It leaves behind
The static mind
Inflames and burns
And its concern
Is not with metric petrifaction
It is of action

It feels
It touches, not conceals
The soul
Which soon congeals
With pedantry galore

Oh, what a bore
To be a slave to meter
And duller still
To face
The petty look
Of commonplace

The Ovaries

The ovaries
They make a subtle but important difference
Oh but we are the same
You and I
Though I long without knowing why
While you have the answers

Life is really simple
ABC
Live, Work and Die
The poor grow poorer
And the rich grow Richer
And wars are in the balance of nature

While I look for depths
In a shallow pan say you
And I strain for music
As the water gurgles down the drain

We are really the same
You and I
But the ovaries
They make a subtle but important difference

The Game

I've learned the game
The small talk
And the careful cultivation
Of ones friends for reasons
The stifling of the seasons inside the breast
For daily order

To talk the language of another country
Without myself inside, only my brain
Is this democracy?
I keep out no one
Yet the heart within is drowned in lies
And memory dies of suffocation

Where's the floating island
That I was, touching sometimes
With another island
Floating free together for awhile?

We are all one now
A thin flat pancake of sincerity
Goodwill, politeness then abounds
And I make friendly sounds -
I've learned the game.

Memories

Why does a warm wind blow in winter

Unexpected
Unbidden
Unawaited

Bringing with it a scent of memory

And promises
Never made
Or hoped for

Breathing the long forgotten breath of summer

A sudden empty joy
Which ends
Before beginning

The Boogey Man

Who is the Boogey Man that waits
In the dark wedge behind the open door
In the house when the footsteps are gone
And the streets silent
In that gaping moment when the chores are done
And the coffee lies stagnant in the cup
And in the silence the mind stirs
Like a sleeping giant
A Pandora's Box phantomly opening on its own
And the shadows seeping out
Slide around like smoke
That smarts and suffocates

Who is the Boogey Man that waits
For the deathly stillness of an empty moment
When the conversation like a worn record
Plays itself again
And words are fed into the air
An endless ticker-tape
Depositing in ever growing reams of waist
On a bare evening

Who is the Boogey Man that waits
For the dark island of your bed
When no one speaks and sleep should come
When all the things you could have been
And should have said and might have done
And all the hearts and bodies you'd have touched
Stand like Poe's "Raven" perched on your memory -
"Nevermore"

Untitled

Why is there such a warmth in me
That finds no exit in the world?
Like an early false start of spring
Trapped by an afterthought of snow -
The earth, ready to exhale her moist release
Surprised to find the cold white touch of reason.

Untitled

Can you bare the pain of lovely music
The birth agony which dies a-borning
The licking flames of memories centuries old
And yet unsurfaced
The imagined lover seen somewhere in childhood
Past master of the look and touch
Of sweetness unendurable

The Radio

The radio radiates
An artificial hothouse of sunshine music
On a cold rainy day
A splash of bright red sound
That stamps around the edges of a gray day.
ZIPPEDY DOO DAH GOOD MORNIN' WORLD
And the rain leaks cold and long
Outside my window

Like false drunk joy
At a dull and endless party
The sound of canned high spirits
(Which you know is in more cans
than Campbell's Pork and Beans
at the local supermarket)
Smacks the loneliness across your face
With a wet towel sting
When before it was just dull and painless

Better Bach
Or better nothing

The Stalwart Knight

The stalwart knight
With his helmet
Down about his neck
Goes onward into battle
Fiercely forward to the fortress
In the blackest night
His sights unseen

Tunneling through forests thick
He gathers speed
And pays no mind
To the rushing wind
On his sturdy steed

And now! A thrust,
A quiver, the target's reached
His triumph's full
And victory with a violence
Bursts the dams
And the overflow
Courses through the furrows

Our knight is done
And resting curled up on a bed of dew
He looks all meekness
As a helpless babe
Tossed like flotsam
On a shining shore

The Teacher

("I Am Good With Unicorns" - Inspired by B.J. McComis)

The children feast on my presence
As winter sparrows at a plate of cake crumbs
And when all is done they go home
To their parents and/or guardians
Sisters brothers aunts and uncles
Cousins first and second
Third once removed -
Family - blood family

"You are good with children"

I am good with -
        unicorns

I have friends
Good friends
To fill a room with party revelers
To ask me home for dinner -
Even friends who'll open up their couch
For one week or two
One month or two

I have friends
Who ask me why I cry
Or better yet don't ask
But wait
In mute acceptance

I have friends
Who call and open up their souls
As willingly as If I had their souls to share
Because my own
Half empty
And disused
Has not been made a claim upon

"You are a warm and honest friend"

I am good
        with
            unicorns

There are things I do
Much praised
They are my presents from and to this world
An auntie bearing gifts
And when she goes the gifts remain
The giver unimportant

And people drink of me
As of an everlasting source
And only I know
If the rain will come again
Or if beneath
There courses still a deeper flow

            "You are an endless fount of strength
            a pillar
            rock
            a mountain of stability"

I am
  good
    with
      unicorns

War

The choice is poison

To set upon your flesh and blood to kill
And say Amen
Or wait for prophecy
Uncertain always because it only prophesies
To prove a still more galling end

To tell your son to mutilate
And send him forth a sacrifice
Of either flesh or soul
Selling his membranes to disembowelment
Or his spirit to a lifetime of damnation
For a postulate

What do we know that history
Has proved a thousand times
The soulless shall inherit the earth
And do we wait ready to barter
Or do we join accepting our inheritance

The choice is poison

On The Closing Of A Show

(Sudden Death)

Strange that; the ending of a play-run,
Like the death of a friend of the parting of a lover,
The between-scene music like "Our Song"
Echoing through the mind.

Accustomed to performance,
Mind and body feels the words and movements
As the amputee senses fingers twitching
On a severed limb;

The strange suffocation of an empty evening,
Empty of place, family -
A life begun and ended without warning.

V Middle Age

To Barbara, Our Teacher*

Why she can reach the small still soul,
The quiet child within us all;
Can touch the simple heart of youth,
The precious voice of inner truth.
In one clear thought, In one clean phrase
She paints the highlight of our days,
She brings the seasons of our past
A clarity to make them last in memory.

And what a vision for our mind,
Those dreams we thought we left behind,
She brings them voice; a song so clear
In words so choice they touch the tissue
Of the inner ear.

Her characters both brave and true
Are little bits of me and you
And of our children whom she guides
To trust the nature of their minds
To her sure hand and surer song,
Leading youthful thoughts along
To their most wonderful completion
As both the teacher and the vision!

*(Written as a tribute to Barbara Cohen,
prize winning author of children's books.)*

Background Music

Some children are like that:
"Oh stop that music - it makes me cry!"
"Don't sing that song, Mommy, it's so sad!"
And these same children listen later
With all their being, and are transformed.
They enter worlds most will never see within a lifetime,
But only when we pass dimension's hallways into other worlds.

Yet a concerto that one soul has snatched from God
Becomes the background blah for nattering and chattering,
And these same children, later grown,
And fearing the totality of soul immersion
Have backed away from privileged passage
And keep at bay intensity
For noisy density.

In Memory of the Miracle: Helen Keller

(This Is God To Me)

How can you talk when you can't hear?
How can you think when you can't see?
What images reach a soundless ear; sound's colors
Splash on vision that can never be?
What is red, purple, gold to a colorless mind -
And how does one think without words' sight?
How do formed fantasies fly their way
Into endless night?

She, who never heard a thought, could read
And write and speak in English,
French, and Greek - a miracle enough
Alone that she could speak!

Explain it to me, if you will, to my tangible sense
How meaning penetrated dense deformity.
Is it simply this; that touch
Can come to mean so much?
Or is it something without mention;
Not of our ken - Divine Intervention?

Suspend Disbelief

Suspend disbelief!
Our Western world's so small.
So limited by facts and figures,
So hemmed in by the gigantic wall
We box our very minds and souls in.
Our future in a small black hole
We live surrounded by the possible,
Accepting only probable.
We see the forest, not the trees,
Our tunnel vision missing the peripheries.
We mole our way through what we think is life
Accepting strife as fact
And miracles as fiction.

Suspend disbelief!
Why better to believe in limitations
Than visitations from a fuller world?
Why ball and chain our intuitions
Allowing inhibitions to vise our creativity?
We plod, not fly, through dreamless days
And laugh at all the crazy ways
Of foreigners and stranger folk
Who do not wear the yoke of black and white.
Those crazy fools, they fly through day -
We slog through night.

Two Worlds

I live in two worlds
Asserting my independence
While assured of my protection
Demanding my independence
Expecting my protection
Insisting on my independence
Accepting my protection

I live in two worlds
I am the master of my body
I go religiously to doctors
I am the master of my soul
I go therapeutically to temples
I am the master of my life
I go dutifully to the polls

I live in two worlds
Acknowledging the spiritual
While dwelling in the material
Aware of infinite reality
While living in the surreal mundane
Attuned to the breakneck racketing of time
While suspended in the gelatinous viscosity
Of endless now

A Footnote to Emily Dickinson's "Success is counted Sweetest"

"OH MY GOD THAT'S WONDERFUL!
HOW GLAD I AM FOR YOU!
IT MAKES ME FEEL SO GOOD
THAT SOMEONE JUST LIKE ME
HAS GOT THE RECOGNITION THAT SHE SHOULD!"

and oh my god it hurts
it's you instead of me
why could you do it and not I
what special gift do you possess
that gives you entry to success

"OH YES, OH YES, THE WORLD IS JUST!
HOW EASILY IT ROLLS -
TWO FOLLOWS ONE AS WELL IT MUST
AND YOU ARE THERE THRUST AFTER THRUST
MOUNTING AS YOUR TRIUMPH TOLLS!"

my days go by like sifting sand
accumulating dunes of dust
I grab each moment as I must
and watch the mounting of the years
while swallowing my deepest fears
that this is how my days will end
a mountain of it-could-have-been

VI Poems of a Mother Tiger
With Her Wounded Cub

The Devil Came Disguised

The devil came disguised as sweet submission
Such soul and hurt and longing in soft fawn eyes
But her memories were drowned in lies
Her list of hurts inflicted
Wants unheeded
Needs restricted
Ah poor gentle creature
Deeply wronged

How many dreams has she destroyed
Her empty parasitic heart has latched once more
Its tentacles of need have found an open door
Until she lays to waste another's life
While crying foul desertion
This gentle perfect wife
Her future in eternal hell
Along with those she's loved so well

The years will pass
And she will find herself bereft
And wronged at every turn
Till at a loss for whom to blame
Still empty and despairing of her shame
She'll visit the same misery
Upon the apple of her womb
As all her life was visited on her

To Her Mother

My child and yours have their just rewards
Their karma within this life shall be realized
He took what was not his to take
She gave what was not hers to give
The sin of their union was unseen by me
But seen by you for the wrongest reasons
Impropriety was your chosen grievance
But the fabric of her life is a tissue of lies
Like a plump fresh onion darkening layer by layer
Till the center discloses a pulp of rot

An Apple Doesn't Fall Far From The Tree

"An apple doesn't fall far from the tree"

I used to think a hurricane blew
The day you dropped from the limb
And scattered your fruit
To the far corners of the world

But now I see the same shape
And substance of your mother trunk
Improved only by the mouth
That bites into you

Anger

Working through the drafts of hatred
Letting the detritus settle to bitter dregs
Leaving a clear surface of light
Good will and what is best for all concerned
That is the work which occupies my mind and soul

Every day the bile surges
Leaving bitter anger in my mouth
But then the ones I love
The refugees of this disaster
Must not be ravaged with the bilge
Their life their love their bright spirit
Shall not be dimmed by my revenge

So slowly slowly does it settle
Never to disappear
But as a flower grows from dung
Peace acceptance and forgiveness
May someday blossom from my ire

VII. Maturity

Reluctant Muses

I feel time's hot breath at my back door
While the muses try to enter gracefully
As I beckon from my front stoop.
They will not be hurried
And my mind balks
Wedged between my persistence
And its natural wont.

How gently they sneak in, these muses
When my back is turned
Though all my feverish beckonings
They spurned!

Looking Back

Lord, oh Lord, wouldn't it be fun
To walk right back into your past,
Take that awkward angry moment
Say the things that you know how to say now,
Do the things you know now can be done.

What rich language you could use, so easily profane;
Treat an insult as a joke,
Make the perpetrator insignificant with one flip gesture,
Barely recognize a threatening name.

Ah, insouciance rare that comes only with distance,
And indifference that comes only with time,
Can take that moment when your enemy triumphed -
Turn frustration to a flippant rhyme.

I Must Not Judge

I must not judge my father
For not admitting he was a Jew
And must not give him excuses
For that is a judgement in itself

He embodied all the Jewish virtues
Although embarrassed by his own people
While I heard Russian prayers
As songs of the Orthodox faith
I also heard the Kol Nidre melody
With such depth and beauty
And an underlying agony
Which to this day brings tears of memory
Of a worship which we never practiced

He was honest
(Though not with himself)
Unfailingly giving
(Though not with his purse)
A nonjudgmental listener
(Though not with his daughter)

He was ashamed of the "Beaten Dog"
Look of the European Jew
And enormously proud of the Israeli
The new arrogant breed
He ran from the one bowed down to the other
Both his Russian and his English were pure Moscow
And not until he had his stroke
Did an alien Ashkenazy Jew invade his speech

I had never questioned that he played
King Ahashuerus at the age of four
And with an actor's pride remembered
His lascivious leer at a juvenile Queen Esther
His pride for the emotion at such an early age
And not the telling of the Megilah
But I always heard the Jew was a special person
A person of gifts and abilities
Of a degree and percentage denied all others

It is so easy to embrace my faith
Without the background of pogroms
Without continual singling out of faults
In a patently brilliant student
Without quotas and exceptions
And pervading hatred and disgust

He entered a new land
That had its own quotas
Where by God or not
That wasn't going to happen anymore

Suicide

Kill yourself and your life is defined by your death
Everything in memory leads to it
I should have known when she said
Remember when he said
The look on her face
What went through his mind when he
When she was a child if that had not happened
When he met her
When she met him
When she was pregnant
His father his mother his brother his child
Her boss her friend her co-worker her sister
Why didn't we do this do that
Not do this not do that
And me me me me
My fault my fault my fault my fault

The memory strains for happy times
For smiles laughter joy and rapture
For quiet times nothing special going on
For conversations not pregnant with burgeoning outcome
Sitting there smoking a cigarette
A book closed on her lap
The smoke curling into the encroaching darkness
Should we have known
Was that a clue

Why do we remember the eyes that visited hell
And not the pleasure at our accomplishments
People tell us there was that
Gentle conversations hang in the memory
But not the voice
We see her face in the mirror
And grief and shock of recognition
Rather than delight

We come across a box of letters
That tell of ordinary times
Or do they
A chronicling of a simple day
Develops a poignant melancholy
That it may never have possessed

Over the years this act of agony unendurable
Becomes an empty anecdote
Or maybe we never really touched it
For to do so would most likely end our reason

We dream she has always been here
Somewhere nearby just out of reach
Just a phone call away but fingers slip off the keys
As we try over and over to touch to hear to see
She's been here all along and I've forgotten
And in my dream I ache I ache

On Aging

She's someone I don't know
But have seen her come and go time and time again
She's mother, grandmother, stranger, friend
Actor, businessperson or a hausfrau
Dumpy, frumpy, groomed, perfumed
Her neck sags, her jowls bag
Or maybe hey that's not too bad
Yet who's this foreigner I see
And what has she to do with me

She turned the corner crossed the street
And years ago left me behind
My mind inhabits someone else
and what she looks like I'm not sure
Perhaps she really has no form
Is just a thought, an essence pure
But truly noting as I pass
She isn't me
That stranger startled staring
From each reflective glass

On Grasping Time

When do we first become aware of this spinning globe called time?
When day-click-night-click-day bumps by
When seasons fly
"Last summer when we...."
No, that was three years ago
And can that really be our little Dave?
It was just yesterday
Just last year - and a decade's gone -
No, make that two -
Didn't I just...
Wasn't that when...
No, that was a long long time ago.

A plane goes by in the purple blue of a frosty night
On a summer night
On an autumn flight
On a springtime promise-of-forever night
A twinkling flashing star gliding by our horizon.
A plane goes by in the purple blue of any night
And while it's there it's bright, so bright
And while it's there it's twinkling light
And disappears into the dark of our horizon.

Ever try to grasp a moment?
Grip your sheets in the pale of a morning
And suddenly feel the whirling earth
So fast your heart pounds, your breath stops
And almost, almost you are flung into insanity?

Live for tomorrow, but tomorrow is always tomorrow
And now slips by unnoticed.
Live for now, but what is now,
Now already was, has been, had been , once had been...
Live, just live, just take it in
And know you take it in, every sound,
Every color, every smell, every taste and touch -
There's just so much!

How do you stop this spinning globe called time?
Don't try - Just let it roll
Just hang on like a fly
Just be.

Your Daughter

I went to your daughter's wedding
I've met her husband and her second son
I've known the fulfilled woman she's become
We speak contemporaries now with time
Over the distances by phone

I find us hedging round your name
Each one afraid to share the pain of loss
I see beginnings of your feathered lines
Around her cobalt eyes a certain toss
Of honeyed hair which so defines
The same arched brow

Where are you now
Your face smiles back at me
From the refrigerator door
I know there must be more somewhere
Somehow beyond the prison of my brain

Who can explain the veil of death
There is no substitute for you
No other friend will do
To give back what we had
But I'm so glad your daughter's near

On Candid Photos

Who the hell is that old bag
With legs no longer slender but sinewy
With lumpy hips, a dowager's pot
Swinging wattles from arms and jaws
A hag's gaping grin
The fillings outnumbering the teeth
Cow-like breasts replacing mountain peaks
With hair an artificial dark
The silver coming up like weeds
An ass just like a bean-bag chair
What is the photo processing
That sends her home to me
She haunts your camera
Like someone's displaced aunt

The Season of Romance

The season of romance has passed somehow
Without my knowing when
The anticipation, the desire
How I miss the fire of the sudden moment of discovery
Intense looks of love in eyes
That visit now only in dreams
It seems I should be satisfied with calmer things

They say each season brings its own reward
But I'm not ready yet for winter
Autumnal colors vibrantly recall
A warmer season in my heart
Which makes it hard to part
With summer memories

Reflection

Long ago is yesterday
And ten years is tomorrow
Time melts and runs and fuses
Joys interweave with sorrow

There's nothing new that can be done
And all that's old is said
And lifetime was before us
Now much of it's been read

The days run through our fingers
Like grasps of sifting sand
Yet still I'm like a baby
With worlds to understand